Fairy ENCHANTMENT

Introduction

There is a special world that we all discover during the tender years of childhood that is filled with fantastic images and wondrous magic. Tales of extraordinary and elusive creatures fill the books we read and take us into a world of unending imagination. As the real world begins to replace the fairy tales we so loved, how fortunate we are when we can still see magic in the flutter of a butterfly's wings or be fascinated by the twinkle of a firefly on a warm summer's evening.

When puttering in the garden or walking through a misty wood, our minds may wonder what might go on when those of us from this earthly realm are not watching. Are there sprites and elves amongst the foxglove and bluebells? Is that rustling of leaves a delicate fairy scurrying out of sight?

Inside this book you will find a delightful array of Joan Elliott's favorite fairies inspired by the natural world she loves so much and the wonderful stories we've all heard and read. Journey with us through the nine designs Joan has created just for you. We will glimpse at a fairy's garden, watch the flight of a precious butterfly fairy, take a magical ride on an elegant dragon, be greeted by a majestic fairy queen, find inspiration in the messages of playful sprites and get to listen in on a favorite story of *Once Upon a Time*.

Butterfly Fairy,
page 8

Once Upon a Time,
page 14

The Fairy Queen,
page 20

House of White Birches, Berne, Indiana 46711   AnniesAttic.com

Meet the Designer

Joan Elliott has been creating needlework designs for close to 40 years. After graduating with a degree in fine arts, Joan's passion for color and interest in fiber art found an easy home in the needlework world. With countless cross-stitch designs to her credit and the many books she has published over the years, her distinctive style is easily recognized and appreciated by cross-stitch enthusiasts around the world.

Joan is a regular contributor to the major cross-stitch magazines in both the United States and the United Kingdom, and kits and chartpacks of her designs are sold worldwide. Working with one of her favorite themes, fairies in cross-stitch, Joan is delighted to bring you all-new designs done exclusively for House of White Birches.

Joan divides her time between New York City and the peaceful countryside of Vermont where she joyfully indulges her passion for gardening and is forever inspired by the beauty of the nature that surrounds her. She and her husband feel truly blessed to share all the joys of both city and country life.

*The Fairy &
the Dragon,*
page 26

A Fairy's Garden,
page 32

Childhood Magic
page 38

House of White Birches, Berne, Indiana 46711 AnniesAttic.com

How to Stitch

Working From Charted Designs

A square on a chart corresponds to a space for a Cross-Stitch on the stitching surface. The symbol in a square shows the floss color to be used for the stitch. The width and height for the design stitch-area are given; centers are shown by arrows. Backstitches are shown by straight lines, and French Knots are shown by dots.

Fabrics

In our Materials listings we give Joan Elliott's fabric suggestions that will complement each design. Our front-cover model was worked on Big bang 28-count hand-dyed Jobelan by Polstitches Designs. Jobelan is an even-weave fabric that has the same number of horizontal and vertical threads (or blocks of threads) per inch. That number is called the thread count.

The size of the design is determined by the size of the even-weave fabric on which you work. Use the chart below as a guide to determine the finished size of a design on various popular sizes of cross-stitch fabric.

Thread	Number of Stitches in Design				
Count	10	20	30	40	50
11-count	1"	1¾"	2¾"	3⅝"	4½"
14-count	¾"	1⅜"	2⅛"	2⅞"	3⅝"
16-count	⅝"	1¼"	1⅞"	2½"	3⅛"
18-count	½"	1⅛"	1⅝"	2¼"	2¾"
25-count	⅜"	⅞"	1¼"	1⅝"	2"
28-count	⅜"	¾"	1"	1⅜"	1¾"
32-count	¼"	⅝"	⅞"	1¼"	1½"

(measurements are given to the nearest ⅛")

Needles

A blunt-tipped tapestry needle, size 24 or 26, is used for stitching on most 14-count to 28-count fabrics. The higher the needle number, the smaller the needle. The correct-size needle is easy to thread with the amount of floss required, but is not so large that it will distort the holes in the fabric. The following chart indicates the appropriate-size needle for each size of fabric, along with the suggested number of strands of floss to use.

Fabric	Strands of Floss	Tapestry Needle Size
11-count	3	24 or 26
14-count	2	24 or 26
16-count	2	24, 26 or 28
18-count	1 or 2	26 or 28
25-count	1	26 or 28
28-count over two threads	2	26 or 28
32-count over two threads	2	28

Floss

Our front-cover model was stitched using DMC six-strand embroidery floss. Color numbers are given for floss. Both DMC and Anchor color numbers are given for each design. Cut floss into comfortable working lengths; we suggest about 18 inches.

Blending Filament & Metallic Braid

Blending filament is a fine, shiny fiber that can be used alone or combined with floss or other thread. Knotting the blending filament on the needle with a slip knot is recommended for control (Fig. 1).

Metallic braid is a braided metallic fiber, usually used single-ply. Thread this fiber just as you would any other fiber. Use short lengths, about 15 inches, to keep the fiber from fraying.

Fig. 1
Slipknot

Getting Started

To begin in an unstitched area, bring threaded needle from back to front of fabric. Hold an inch of the end against the back, and then hold it in place with your first few stitches. To end threads and begin new ones next to existing stitches, weave through the backs of several stitches.

The Stitches

The number of strands used for Cross-Stitches will be determined by the thread count of the fabric used. Refer to the Needles chart to determine the number of strands used for Cross-Stitches. Use one strand for Backstitches.

Cross-Stitch

The Cross-Stitch is formed in two motions. Follow the numbering in Fig. 2 and bring needle up at 1, down at 2, up at 3 and down at 4 to complete the stitch. Work horizontal rows of stitches (Fig. 3) wherever possible. Bring thread up at 1, work half of each stitch across the row, and then complete the stitches on your return.

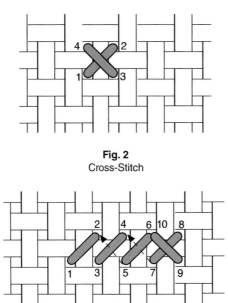

Fig. 2
Cross-Stitch

Fig. 3
Cross-Stitch
Horizontal Row

Half Cross-Stitch

The first part of a Cross-Stitch may slant in either direction (Fig. 4).

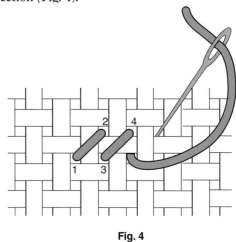

Fig. 4
Half Cross-Stitch

Backstitch

Backstitches are worked after Cross-Stitches have been completed. They may slope in any direction and are occasionally worked over more than one square of fabric. Fig. 5 shows the progression of several stitches; bring thread up at odd numbers and down at even numbers. Frequently, you must choose where to end one Backstitch color and begin the next color. Choose the object that should appear closest to you. Backstitch around that shape with the appropriate color, and then Backstitch the areas behind it with adjacent color(s).

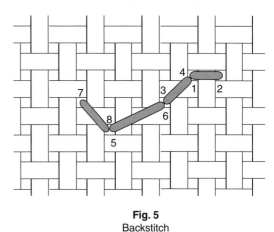

Fig. 5
Backstitch

House of White Birches, Berne, Indiana 46711 AnniesAttic.com

Quarter Stitch

The Quarter Stitch is formed in one motion. Follow the numbering in Fig. 6 and bring needle up at 1 and down at 2. The Quarter Stitch is used to fill in small spaces in the design where there is not enough room for a full stitch.

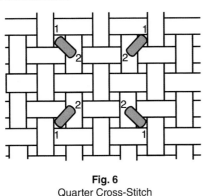

Fig. 6
Quarter Cross-Stitch

French Knot

Bring thread up where indicated on chart. Wrap floss once around needle (Fig. 7) and reinsert needle at 2, close to 1, but at least one fabric thread away from it. Hold wrapping thread tightly and pull needle through, letting thread go just as knot is formed. For a larger knot, use more strands of floss.

Fig. 7
French Knot

Stitching With Beads

Small seed beads can be added to any cross-stitch design, using one bead per stitch. Knot thread at beginning of beaded section for security, especially if you are adding beads to clothing. The bead should lie in the same direction as the top half of cross-stitches.

Bead Attachment

Use one strand of floss to secure beads. Bring beading needle up from back of work (Fig. 8), leaving a 2-inch length of thread hanging; do not knot (end will be secured between stitches as you work). Thread bead on needle; complete stitch.

Do not skip over more than two stitches or spaces without first securing thread, or last bead will be loose. To secure, weave thread into several stitches on back of work. Follow graph to work design, using one bead per stitch.

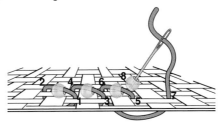

Fig. 8
Bead Attachment

Planning a Project

Before you stitch, decide how large to cut fabric. Determine the stitched size and then allow enough additional fabric around the design plus 4 inches more on each side for use in finishing and mounting.

Cut your fabric exactly true, right along the holes of the fabric. Some raveling may occur as you handle the fabric. To minimize raveling along the raw edges, use an overcast basting stitch, machine zigzag-stitch or masking tape, which you can cut away when you are finished.

Finishing Needlework

When you have finished stitching, dampen your embroidery (or, if soiled, wash in lukewarm mild soapsuds and rinse well). Roll in a towel to remove excess moisture. Place facedown on a dry towel or padded surface; press carefully until dry and smooth. Make sure all thread ends are well anchored and clipped closely. Proceed with desired finishing.

Butterfly Fairy

The soft misty sky of a midsummer's dawn is the perfect backdrop for the Butterfly Fairy. Lifted by her delicate wings, she dances in a joyful celebration with her tiny friends by her side.

Materials

- Big bang 28-count hand-dyed Jobelan*: 19 x 22 inches
- Six-strand floss as indicated in color key
- Kreinik very fine (#4) braid as indicated in color key

Butterfly Fairy was stitched on big bang 28-count hand-dyed Jobelan from Polstitches Designs, using DMC floss and Kreinik braid. Finished piece was custom framed.

Skill Level

Easy

Stitch Count

147 wide x 194 high

Approximate Design Size

- 11-count 13⅜" x 17⅝"
- 14-count 10½" x 13⅞"
- 16-count 9¼" x 12⅛"
- 18-count 8⅛" x 10¾"
- 25-count 5⅞" x 7¾"
- 28-count over 2 threads 10½" x 13⅞"
- 32-count over 2 threads 9¼" x 12⅛"

Instructions

Center and stitch design on 28-count Jobelan, working over 2 threads. Use 2 strands floss or 1 strand Kreinik braid for full, half and quarter Cross-Stitch; 1 strand floss or Kreinik braid for all Backstitch; and 2 strands floss or 1 strand Kreinik braid, wrapped once, for French Knot.

FULL, HALF & QUARTER CROSS-STITCH (2X)

DMC		ANCHOR	COLORS
1	○	2	White
165	∼	293	Very light moss green
166	⚐	279	Medium light moss green
340	⌘	118	Medium blue violet
524	=	858	Very light fern green
729	★	890	Medium old gold
742	◓	303	Light tangerine
743	⌀	302	Medium yellow
744	I	301	Pale yellow
938	◣	381	Ultra dark coffee brown
945	☆	881	Tawny
951	⽊	1010	Light tawny
3053	◿	261	Green gray
3350	♥	59	Ultra dark dusty rose
3746	↓	1030	Dark blue violet
3747	♡	1020	Very light blue violet
3752	⫷	1032	Very light antique blue
3753	◥	1031	Ultra very light antique blue
3770	▷	1009	Very light tawny
3829	✿	901	Very dark old gold
3838	✳	177	Dark lavender blue
3839	✂	176	Medium lavender blue
3840	∽	117	Light lavender blue

FULL, HALF & QUARTER CROSS-STITCH (1X)

KREINIK VERY FINE (#4) BRAID		COLORS
045	m	Confetti gold
5008	▲	Leprechaun
5982	♣	Forest green

BACKSTITCH (1X)

DMC		ANCHOR	COLORS
433	—	358	Medium brown (chin, eyebrows)
938	—	381	Ultra dark coffee brown* (face, body/clothing)
3350	—	59	Ultra dark dusty rose* (lips)

KREINIK VERY FINE (#4) BRAID		COLORS
045	—	Confetti gold* (fairy wings, detail on dress bodice; butterfly wings)
5008	—	Leprechaun* (fairy antennae; 3 butterfly antennae and tails)
5982	—	Forest green* (flowers in hair, vines; 4 butterfly antennae and tails)

FRENCH KNOT (2X)

DMC		ANCHOR	COLOR
1	●	2	White* (dress bodice)

FRENCH KNOT (1X)

KREINIK VERY FINE (#4) BRAID		COLOR
5008	●	Leprechaun*
5982	●	Forest green*

*Duplicate color

House of White Birches, Berne, Indiana 46711   AnniesAttic.com

House of White Birches, Berne, Indiana 46711 AnniesAttic.com

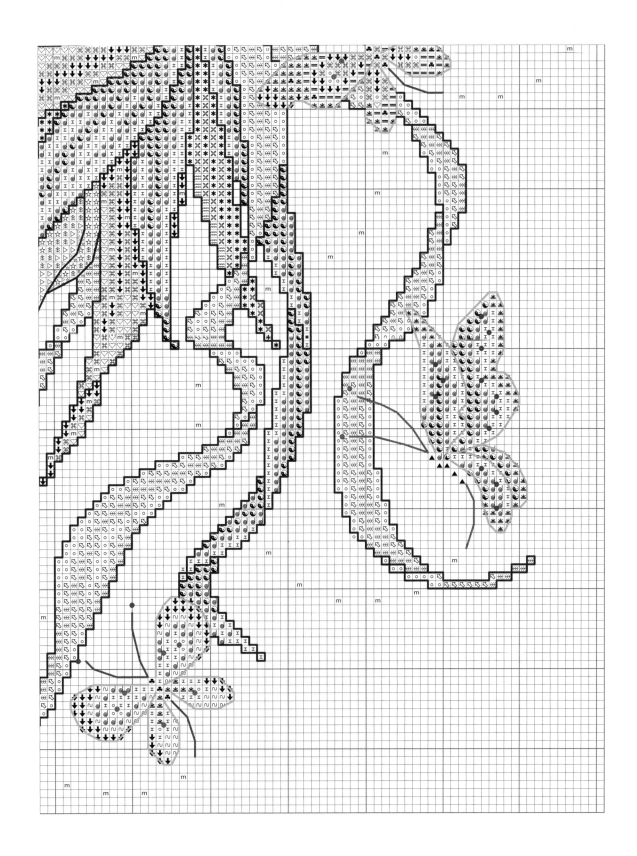

Once Upon a Time

Hush now ... it is that special time when even fairy mothers can share a quiet moment with their little ones. The book is open, the scene is set with visions of mysterious castles and wonderful adventures, and so she begins, "Once upon a time ..."

Materials

- Fairy dreams 28-count hand-dyed Jobelan*: 20 x 24 inches
- Six-strand floss as indicated in color key
- Kreinik very fine (#4) braid as indicated in color key
- Mill Hill glass seed beads: G00374 rainbow, G02031 citron

Fairy dreams 28-count hand-dyed Jobelan is available from Polstitches Designs.

Skill Level

Easy

Stitch Count

168 wide x 221 high

Approximate Design Size

- 11-count 15¼" x 20"
- 14-count 12" x 15¾"
- 16-count 10½" x 13⅞"
- 18-count 9⅜" x 12¼"
- 25-count 6¾" x 8⅞"
- 28-count over 2 threads 12" x 15¾"
- 32-count over 2 threads 10½" x 13⅞"

Instructions

Center and stitch design on 28-count Jobelan, working over 2 threads. Use 2 strands floss or 1 strand Kreinik braid for full, half and quarter Cross-Stitch; 1 strand floss or Kreinik braid for all Backstitch; and 2 strands floss or 1 strand Kreinik braid, wrapped once, for French Knot. Attach bead with 1 strand coordinating-color floss.

FULL, HALF & QUARTER CROSS-STITCH (2X)

DMC		ANCHOR	COLORS
1	⋈	2	White
155		109	Medium dark blue violet
341	✦	117	Light blue violet
471	✚	266	Very light avocado green
472	▦	253	Ultra light avocado green
676	C	891	Light old gold
677	✕	886	Very light old gold
729	◩	890	Medium old gold
746	~	275	Off-white
801	8	359	Dark coffee brown
869	⚓	944	Very dark hazelnut brown
902	●	897	Very dark garnet
912	↓	209	Light emerald green
926	◔	850	Medium gray green
927	♣	848	Light gray green
938	■	381	Ultra dark coffee brown
945	◈	881	Tawny
951	◩	1010	Light tawny
954	✚	203	Nile green
955	☐	206	Light Nile green
3346	✿	267	Hunter green
3687	♠	68	Mauve
3746	◉	1030	Dark blue violet
3747	◉	1020	Very light blue violet
3752	✳	1032	Very light antique blue
3753	╱	1031	Ultra very light antique blue
3768	♥	779	Dark gray green
3770	⇨	1009	Very light tawny
3803	◉	972	Dark mauve
3829	◆	901	Very dark old gold
3834	▣	100	Dark grape
3835	◢	98	Medium grape
3836	✕	90	Light grape

CROSS-STITCH (1X)

KREINIK VERY FINE (#4) BRAID		COLORS
025	▣	Gray
028	◀	Citron

BACKSTITCH STITCH (1X)

DMC		ANCHOR	COLORS
801	—	359	Dark coffee brown* (adult fairy eyebrows, nose, face; child fairy nose, chin; flag poles)
869	—	944	Very dark hazelnut brown* (child fairy forehead)
938	—	381	Ultra dark coffee brown* (Adult and child fairy bodies/clothing, eyes; child fairy side of face; book pages, lettering)
3803	—	972	Dark mauve* (lips)

KREINIK VERY FINE (#4) BRAID		COLORS
025	—	Gray* (adult fairy wings)
028	—	Citron* (child fairy wings; detail on adult fairy dress and hair)

House of White Birches, Berne, Indiana 46711   AnniesAttic.com

FRENCH KNOT (2X)

DMC	ANCHOR	COLOR
938 ●	381	Ultra dark coffee brown*

FRENCH KNOT (1X)

KREINIK VERY	
FINE (#4) BRAID	COLOR
028 ●	Citron*

ATTACH BEAD

MILL HILL GLASS	
SEED	COLORS
G00374 ●	Rainbow
G02031 ●	Citron

*Duplicate color

House of White Birches, Berne, Indiana 46711 AnniesAttic.com

House of White Birches, Berne, Indiana 46711   AnniesAttic.com

House of White Birches, Berne, Indiana 46711 AnniesAttic.com

The Fairy Queen

Set atop her toadstool throne, the elegant Queen of the Fairies casts her spell across her magical realm. Her gossamer wings and golden crown reflect the dappled light beams that filter through to the forest floor.

Materials

- Daybreak 28-count hand-dyed Jobelan*: 20 x 24 inches
- Six-strand floss as indicated in color key
- Kreinik very fine (#4) braid as indicated in color key

Daybreak 28-count hand-dyed Jobelan is available from Polstiches Designs.

Skill Level

Easy

Stitch Count

160 wide x 219 high

Approximate Design Size

- 11-count 14½" x 20"
- 14-count 11⅜" x 15⅝"
- 16-count 10" x 13¾"
- 18-count 8⅞" x 12⅛"
- 22-count 7¼" x 10"
- 25-count 6⅜" x 8¾"
- 28-count over 2 threads 11⅜" x 15⅝"
- 32-count over 2 threads 10" x 13¾"

Instructions

Center and stitch design on 28-count Jobelan, working over 2 threads. Use 2 strands floss or 1 strand Kreinik braid for full, half and quarter Cross-Stitch; 1 strand floss or braid for all Backstitch; and 1 strand Kreinik braid, wrapped once, for French Knot.

FULL, HALF & QUARTER CROSS-STITCH (2X)

DMC		ANCHOR	COLORS
1	○	2	White
153	♡	342	Very light violet
155	∭	109	Medium dark blue violet
166	∪	279	Medium light moss green
167	★	375	Very dark yellow beige
333	❽	119	Very dark blue violet
554	♦♦	96	Very light violet
581	♣	280	Moss green
677	◈	886	Very light old gold
680	▶	901	Dark old gold
746	▷	275	Off-white
869	◢	944	Very dark hazelnut brown
927	☆	848	Light gray green
928	⚡	274	Very light gray green
945	✳	881	Tawny
951	⑤	1010	Light tawny
975	◆	355	Dark golden brown
976	◰	1001	Medium golden brown
977	?	1002	Light golden brown
3022	▲	8581	Medium brown gray
3023	▨	1040	Light brown gray
3024	⚛	397	Very light brown gray
3746	▣	1030	Dark blue violet
3770	∧	1009	Very light tawny
3799	●	236	Very dark pewter gray
3803	♥	972	Dark mauve
3819	≪	278	Light moss green
3821	❀	305	Straw
3847	✖	1076	Dark teal green
3848	☁	1074	Medium teal green
3849	═	1070	Light teal green
3852	✺	306	Very dark straw

FULL, HALF & QUARTER CROSS-STITCH (1X)

KREINIK VERY FINE (#4) BRAID		COLORS
015	⌘	Chartreuse
028	m	Citron
3260	e	Gold tourmaline
5003	↓	Dragonfly

BACKSTITCH (1X)

DMC		ANCHOR	COLORS
869	—	944	Very dark hazelnut brown* (eyebrows, nose, lower face)
3799	—	236	Very dark pewter gray* (eyes, face, body/clothes)
3803	—	972	Dark mauve* (lips)

KREINIK VERY FINE (#4) BRAID		COLORS
015	—	Chartreuse* (leaves, vines, detail on skirt)
028	—	Citron* (necklace; wings)
3260	—	Gold tourmaline* (detail on bodice)
5003	—	Dragonfly* (butterfly)

FRENCH KNOT (1X)

KREINIK VERY FINE (#4) BRAID		COLORS
028	●	Citron*
5003	●	Dragonfly*

*Duplicate color

House of White Birches, Berne, Indiana 46711   AnniesAttic.com

House of White Birches, Berne, Indiana 46711 AnniesAttic.com

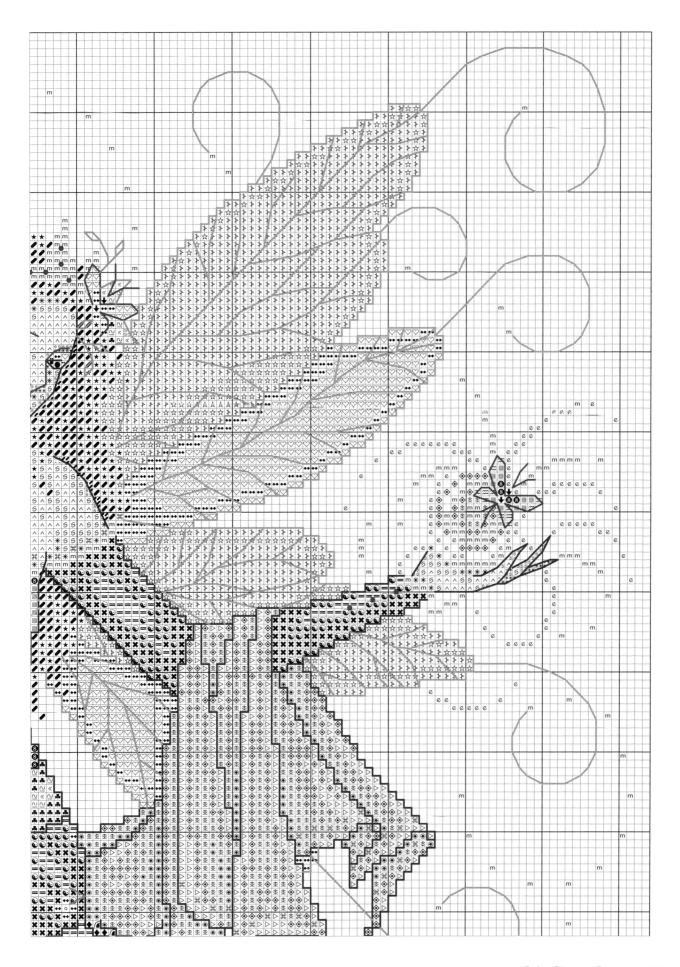

House of White Birches, Berne, Indiana 46711 AnniesAttic.com

The Fairy & the Dragon

With wings shimmering in the light and her pretty skirt flowing in the breeze, a petite dark-haired sprite perches safely on a most elegant dragon. His powerful wings let them soar high as they travel far above their fairyland home.

Materials

- Forrest queen 28-count hand-dyed Jobelan*: 20 x 24 inches
- Six-strand floss as indicated in color key
- Kreinik very fine (#4) braid as indicated in color key

Forrest queen 28-count hand-dyed Jobelan is available from Polstitches Designs.

Skill Level

Easy

Stitch Count

165 wide x 219 high

Approximate Design Size

11-count 15" x 20"
14-count 11¾" x 15¾"
16-count 10½" x 13⅝"
18-count 9⅛" x 12⅛"
25-count 6⅝" x 8¾"
28-count over 2 threads 11¾" x 15¾"
32-count over 2 threads 10½" x 13⅝"

Instructions

Center and stitch design on 28-count Jobelan, working over 2 threads. Use 2 strands floss or 1 strand Kreinik braid for full, half and quarter Cross-Stitch; 1 strand floss or Kreinik braid for all Backstitch; and 2 strands floss or 1 strand Kreinik braid, wrapped once, for French Knot.

FULL, HALF & QUARTER CROSS-STITCH (2X)

DMC		ANCHOR	COLORS
1	○	2	White
150	♥	57	Ultra very dark dusty rose
157	≋	120	Very light cornflower blue
310	●	403	Black
368	⚓	214	Light green pistachio
369	⬡	1043	Very light pistachio green
415	?	398	Pearl gray
501	♣	878	Dark blue green
502	⌣	877	Blue green
503	«	876	Medium blue green
780	±	309	Ultra very dark topaz
782	◱	307	Dark topaz
783	#	306	Medium topaz
792	▼	941	Dark cornflower blue
793	✳	176	Medium cornflower blue
794	$	175	Light cornflower blue
801	◢	359	Dark coffee brown
830	✿	277	Dark golden olive
831	⊛	277	Medium golden olive
833	☆	907	Light golden olive
927	☽	848	Light gray green
928	⬦	274	Very light gray green
938	◆	381	Ultra dark coffee brown
945	✕	881	Tawny
951	▽	1010	Light tawny
3350	⌘	59	Ultra dark dusty rose
3731	+	76	Very dark dusty rose
3733	♡	75	Dusty rose
3770	◿	1009	Very light tawny

FULL, HALF & QUARTER CROSS-STITCH (1X)

KREINIK VERY FINE (#4) BRAID		COLORS
015	⍟	Chartreuse
025	❽	Gray

BACKSTITCH (1X)

DMC		ANCHOR	COLORS
310	—	403	Black* (dragon head, body; fairy eyes, left face, body/clothing)
801	—	359	Dark coffee brown* (fairy right face, nostrils, eyebrows)
3350	—	59	Ultra dark dusty rose* (fairy lips)

KREINIK VERY FINE (#4) BRAID		COLORS
015	—	Chartreuse* (fairy wings; dragon flourishes)
025	—	Gray* (dragon wings; fairy necklace)
028	—	Citron (dragon face, flourishes, scales; fairy hair)

FRENCH KNOT (2X)

DMC		ANCHOR	COLOR
1	●	2	White* (dragon's eye)

FRENCH KNOT (1X)

KREINIK VERY FINE (#4) BRAID		COLOR
028	●	Citron*

*Duplicate color

House of White Birches, Berne, Indiana 46711   AnniesAttic.com

House of White Birches, Berne, Indiana 46711 AnniesAttic.com

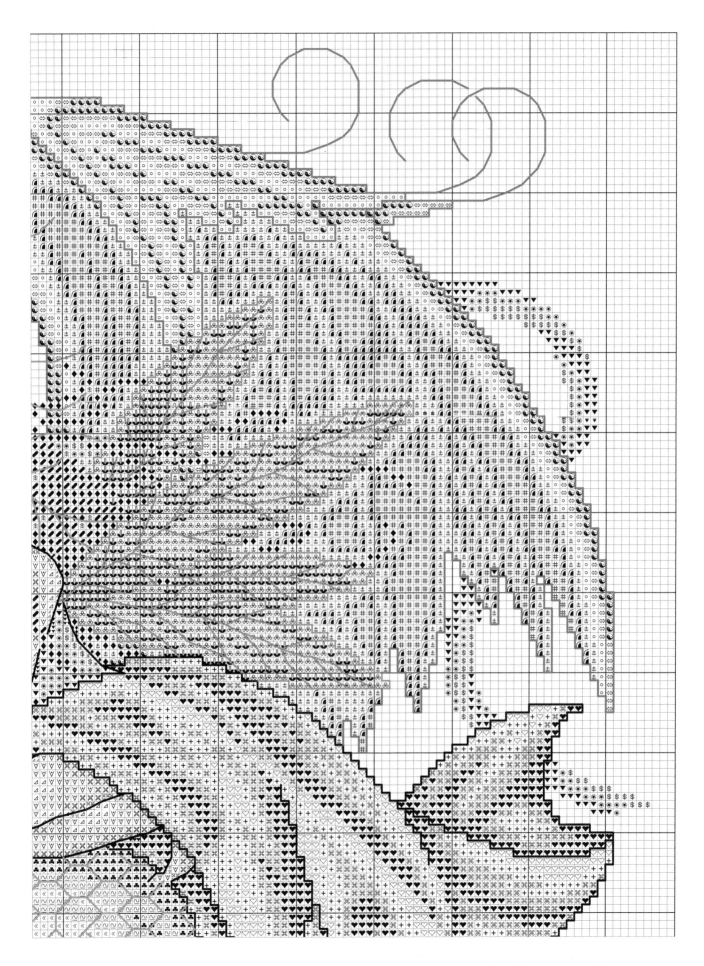

A Fairy's Garden

Who is it that tends the secret gardens and nurtures their fascinating beauty in the wee hours? Surrounded by sheltering foxglove, stately delphinium, nodding mushrooms and colorful primroses, an enchanted fairy tends her shady woodland hideaway.

Materials

- Lavender sunset 28-count Jobelan*:
  19 x 22 inches
- Six-strand floss as indicated in color key
- Kreinik very fine (#4) braid as indicated in color key
- Kreinik fine (#8) braid as indicated in color key

Lavender sunset #429506 28-count Jobelan is available from Wichelt Imports.

Skill Level

Easy

Stitch Count

154 wide x 194 high

Approximate Design Size

11-count 14" x 17⅝"
14-count 11" x 13⅞"
16-count 9⅝" x 12⅛"
18-count 8½" x 10¾"
25-count 6¼" x 7¾"
28-count over 2 threads 11" x 13⅞"
32-count over 2 threads 9⅝" x 12⅛"

Instructions

Center and stitch design on 28-count Jobelan, working over 2 threads. Use 2 strands floss or 1 strand Kreinik braid for full, half and quarter Cross-Stitch; 1 strand floss or Kreinik braid for all Backstitch; and 2 strands floss, wrapped once, for French Knot.

FULL, HALF & QUARTER CROSS-STITCH (2X)

DMC		ANCHOR	COLORS
1	○	2	White
164	a	1042	Light forest green
208	◪	110	Very dark lavender
209	✖	109	Dark lavender
210	C	108	Medium lavender
333	✦✦	119	Very dark blue violet
340	←	118	Medium blue violet
341	✚	117	Light blue violet
433	❽	358	Medium brown
472	8	253	Ultra light avocado green
640	✿	903	Very dark beige gray
644	⊠⊠	830	Medium beige gray
676	✵	891	Light old gold
677	♡	886	Very light old gold
746	⟩	275	Off-white
818	✛	23	Baby pink
832	⊌	907	Golden olive
833	≪	907	Light golden olive
938	◼	381	Ultra dark coffee brown
945	△	881	Tawny
951	∨	1010	Light tawny
975	●	355	Dark golden brown
976	⌘	1001	Medium golden brown
977	⑤	1002	Light golden brown
986	♣	246	Very dark forest green
987	➔	244	Dark forest green
989	⚒	242	Forest green
3023	✾	1040	Light brown gray
3687	◀	68	Mauve
3688	⋘	66	Medium mauve
3746	▰	1030	Dark blue violet
3770	∧	1009	Very light tawny
3803	♥	972	Dark mauve
3820	⊞	306	Dark straw
3822	△	295	Light straw
3852	★	306	Very dark straw

FULL, HALF & QUARTER CROSS-STITCH (1X)

KREINIK FINE (#8) BRAID		COLORS
070	⊞	Mardi gras

KREINIK VERY FINE (#4) BRAID		COLORS
202HL	m	Aztec gold Hi Lustre

BACKSTITCH (1X)

DMC		ANCHOR	COLORS
433	—	358	Medium brown* (eyebrows, nose, flowers)
938	—	381	Ultra dark coffee brown* (face, body/clothing, eyes, mushrooms)
975	—	355	Dark golden brown* (hair strands)
986	—	246	Very dark forest green* (leaves)
3803	—	972	Dark mauve* (lips)

KREINIK FINE (#8) BRAID		COLORS
070	—	Mardi gras

KREINIK VERY FINE (#4) BRAID		COLORS
202HL	—	Aztec gold Hi Lustre

FRENCH KNOT (2X)

DMC		ANCHOR	COLORS
1	●	2	White* (dress bodice)
986	●	246	Very dark forest green*

*Duplicate color

A Fairy's Garden - 33

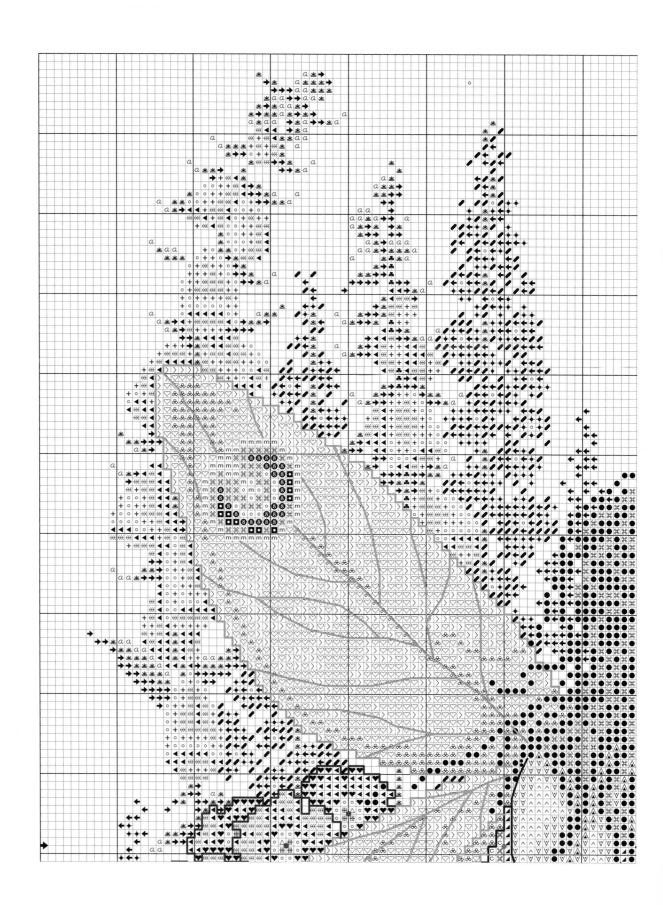

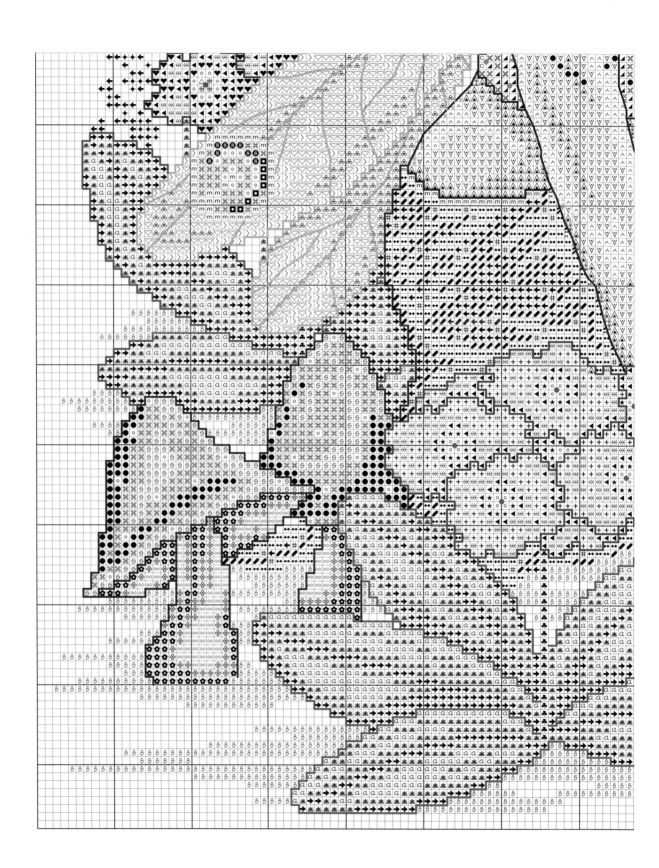

House of White Birches, Berne, Indiana 46711   AnniesAttic.com

Childhood Magic

Four wee fairies carry small bouquets of whimsical flowers and inspiring messages to all who will listen. Their simple words carry us into a world of joy as they remind us to Believe, Dream, Imagine and, of course ... Make A Wish!

House of White Birches, Berne, Indiana 46711   AnniesAttic.com

Imagine . . .

Jump for joy! This sweet fairy has come with her fluttering friends in tow to help set your creative spirit free and imagine that all things are possible.

Materials

- Fairy dust 28-count Cashel linen*: 12½ x 12½ inches
- Six-strand floss as indicated in color key
- Kreinik very fine (#4) braid as indicated in color key

Fairy dust 28-count Cashel linen is available from Zweigart.

Skill Level

Easy

Stitch Count

63 wide x 63 high

Approximate Design Size

11-count 5¾" x 5¾"
14-count 4½" x 4½"
16-count 4" x 4"
18-count 3½" x 3½"
25-count 2½" x 2½"
28-count over 2 threads 4½" x 4½"
32-count over 2 threads 4" x 4"

Instructions

Center and stitch design on 28-count Cashel linen, working over 2 threads. Use 2 strands floss for full, half and quarter Cross-Stitch; 1 strand floss or Kreinik braid for all Backstitch; and 2 strands floss or 1 strand Kreinik braid, wrapped once, for French Knot.

House of White Birches, Berne, Indiana 46711 AnniesAttic.com

FULL, HALF & QUARTER CROSS-STITCH (2X)

DMC		ANCHOR	COLORS
1	○	2	White
208	◖	110	Very dark lavender
209	≋	109	Dark lavender
597	▲	1064	Turquoise
598	◔	1062	Light turquoise
602	♥	63	Medium cranberry
603	✳	62	Cranberry
605	♡	1094	Very light cranberry
742	★	303	Light tangerine
743	△	302	Medium yellow
906	♣	256	Medium parrot green
907	⌐	255	Light parrot green
918	◕	341	Dark red copper
938	●	381	Ultra dark coffee brown
951	∞	1010	Light tawny
3811	⟩	1060	Very light turquoise

BACKSTITCH (1X)

DMC		ANCHOR	COLORS
602	—	63	Medium cranberry* (lips)
938	—	381	Ultra dark coffee brown* (fairy eyes, face, body/clothing; dragonfly body; hat; "Imagine …")

KREINIK VERY FINE (#4) BRAID		COLORS
028	—	Citron (fairy wings; hat brim, tip)
5982	—	Forest green (vines, leaves, border)

FRENCH KNOT (2X)

DMC		ANCHOR	COLOR
938	●	381	Ultra dark coffee brown*

FRENCH KNOT (1X)

KREINIK VERY FINE (#4) BRAID		COLOR
028	●	Citron*

*Duplicate color

Make a Wish!

A bright little pixie flies in on a breeze and brings you a special gift. With a swish of her magical blossoms and a mischievous twinkle in her eye she asks you to make a wish.

Materials

- Little Boy Blue 28-count Laguna linen*: 12½ x 12½ inches
- Six-strand floss as indicated in color key
- Kreinik very fine (#4) braid as indicated in color key

Little Boy Blue 28-count Laguna linen is available from Zweigart.

Skill Level

Easy

Stitch Count

63 wide x 63 high

Approximate Design Size

11-count 5¾" x 5¾"
14-count 4½" x 4½"
16-count 4" x 4"
18-count 3½" x 3½"
25-count 2½" x 2½"
28-count over 2 threads 4½" x 4½"
32-count over 2 threads 4" x 4"

Instructions

Center and stitch design on 28-count Laguna linen, working over 2 threads. Use 2 strands floss for full, half and quarter Cross-Stitch; 1 strand floss or Kreinik braid for all Backstitch; and 2 strands floss or 1 strand Kreinik braid, wrapped once, for French Knot.

FULL, HALF & QUARTER CROSS-STITCH (2X)

DMC		ANCHOR	COLORS
1	○	2	White
208		110	Very dark lavender
209	≋	109	Dark lavender
597	▲	1064	Turquoise
598		1062	Light turquoise
602	♥	63	Medium cranberry
603	✳	62	Cranberry
605	♡	1094	Very light cranberry
742	★	303	Light tangerine
743	△	302	Medium yellow
801	◢	359	Dark coffee brown
906	♣	256	Medium parrot green
938	●	381	Ultra dark coffee brown
951	∞	1010	Light tawny
3811	⟩	1060	Very light turquoise

BACKSTITCH (1X)

DMC		ANCHOR	COLORS
602	—	63	Medium cranberry* (lips)
938	—	381	Ultra dark coffee brown* (fairy eyes, face, body/clothing, hat; dragonfly body; "Make a Wish!")

KREINIK VERY FINE (#4) BRAID | COLORS
| 028 | — | | Citron (fairy wings; hat brim, tip) |
| 5982 | — | | Forest green (vines, leaves, border) |

FRENCH KNOT (2X)

DMC		ANCHOR	COLOR
938	●	381	Ultra dark coffee brown* (fairy eyes, dot on fairy cap, dragonfly head, dot on exlamation point)

FRENCH KNOT (1X)
KREINIK VERY FINE (#4) BRAID | COLOR
| 028 | ● | | Citron* |

*Duplicate color

Believe!

A cheerful sprite, pretty in pink, brings a festive bright garland of wildflowers, fresh picked from the meadow, and encourages us all to believe.

Materials

- Mint green 28-count Cashel linen*: 12½ x 12½ inches
- Six-strand floss as indicated in color key
- Kreinik very fine (#4) braid as indicated in color key

Mint green 28-count Cashel linen is available from Zweigart.

Skill Level

Easy

Stitch Count

63 wide x 63 high

Approximate Design Size

11-count 5¾" x 5¾"
14-count 4½" x 4½"
16-count 4" x 4"
18-count 3½" x 3½"
25-count 2½" x 2½"
28-count over 2 threads 4½" x 4½"
32-count over 2 threads 4" x 4"

Instructions

Center and stitch design on 28-count Cashel linen, working over 2 threads. Use 2 strands floss for full, half and quarter Cross-Stitch; 1 strand floss or Kreinik braid for all Backstitch; and 2 strands floss or 1 strand Kreinik braid, wrapped once, for French Knot.

FULL, HALF & QUARTER CROSS-STITCH (2X)

DMC		ANCHOR	COLORS
1	○	2	White
208	◢	110	Very dark lavender
209	≋	109	Dark lavender
334	✿	997	Medium baby blue
597	▲	1064	Turquoise
598	◉	1062	Light turquoise
602	♥	63	Medium cranberry
603	✳	62	Cranberry
605	♡	1094	Very light cranberry
742	★	303	Light tangerine
743	△	302	Medium yellow
906	♣	256	Medium parrot green
907	∾	2555	Light parrot green
938	●	381	Ultra dark coffee brown
951	∞	1010	Light tawny
3755	🐜	140	Baby blue
3811	⟩	1060	Very light turquoise
3829	⑤	901	Very dark old gold

BACKSTITCH (1X)

DMC		ANCHOR	COLORS
602	—	63	Medium cranberry* (lips)
938	—	381	Ultra dark coffee brown* (fairy eyes, face, body/clothing; dragonfly body; "Believe!")

KREINIK VERY FINE (#4) BRAID   **COLORS**

028	—	Citron (fairy wings; hat brim, tip)
5982	—	Forest green (vines, leaves, border)

FRENCH KNOT (2X)

DMC		ANCHOR	COLOR
938	●	381	Ultra dark coffee brown*

FRENCH KNOT (1X)
KREINIK VERY FINE (#4) BRAID   **COLOR**

028	●	Citron*

*Duplicate color

Dream

It may be as you rest your head on the pillow in the still night or at any quiet daytime moment, but wherever you are this little darling will help make your dreams come true.

Materials
- Bo Peep pink 28-count Cashel linen*: 12½ x 12½ inches
- Six-strand floss as indicated in color key
- Kreinik very fine (#4) braid as indicated in color key

Bo Peep pink 28-count Cashel linen is available from Wichelt Imports.

Skill Level
Easy

Stitch Count
63 wide x 63 high

Approximate Design Size
11-count 5¾" x 5¾"
14-count 4½" x 4½"
16-count 4" x 4"
18-count 3½" x 3½"
25-count 2½" x 2½"
28-count over 2 threads 4½" x 4½"
32-count over 2 threads 4" x 4"

Instructions
Center and stitch design on 28-count Cashel linen, working over 2 threads. Use 2 strands floss for full, half and quarter Cross-Stitch; 1 strand floss or Kreinik braid for all Backstitch; and 2 strands floss or 1 strand Kreinik braid, wrapped once, for French Knot.

House of White Birches, Berne, Indiana 46711   AnniesAttic.com

FULL, HALF & QUARTER CROSS-STITCH (2X)

DMC		ANCHOR	COLORS
1	○	2	White
208	◪	110	Very dark lavender
209	∼	109	Dark lavender
334	✿	997	Medium baby blue
597	▲	1064	Turquoise
598	◕	1062	Light turquoise
602	♥	63	Medium cranberry
603	✳	62	Cranberry
605	♡	1094	Very light cranberry
742	★	303	Light tangerine
743	△	302	Medium yellow
906	♣	256	Medium parrot green
907	∾	255	Light parrot green
938	●	381	Ultra dark coffee brown
951	∞	1010	Light tawny
3755	✾	140	Baby blue
3811	⟩	1060	Very light turquoise

BACKSTITCH (1x)

DMC		ANCHOR	COLORS
602	—	63	Medium cranberry* (lips)
938	—	381	Ultra dark coffee brown* (fairy eyes, face, body/clothing, hat; dragonfly body; "Dream")

KREINIK VERY FINE (#4) BRAID		COLORS
028	—	Citron (fair wings; hat brim, tip)
5982	—	Forest green (vines, leaves, border)

FRENCH KNOT (2X)

DMC		ANCHOR	COLOR
938	●	381	Ultra dark coffee brown*

FRENCH KNOT (1X)

KREINIK VERY FINE (#4) BRAID		COLOR
028	●	Citron*

*Duplicate color

HOUSE of WHITE BIRCHES
PUBLISHERS SINCE 1947

Fairy Enchantment is published by DRG, 306 East Parr Road, Berne, IN 46711. Printed in USA. Copyright © 2011 DRG. All rights reserved. This publication may not be reproduced in part or in whole without written permission from the publisher.

RETAIL STORES: If you would like to carry this pattern book or any other DRG publications, visit DRGwholesale.com

Every effort has been made to ensure that the instructions in this publication are complete and accurate. We cannot, however, take responsibility for human error, typographical mistakes or variations in individual work. Please visit AnniesCustomerCare.com to check for pattern updates.

STAFF

Editor: Barb Sprunger
Technical Editor: Marla Laux
Copy Supervisor: Deborah Morgan
Copy Editors: Emily Carter,
Samantha Schneider
Production Artist Supervisor:
Erin Brandt
Graphic Artists: Glenda Chamberlain,
Jessi Butler

Creative Director: Brad Snow
Assistant Art Director: Nick Pierce
Photography Supervisor:
Tammy Christian
Photography: Matthew Owen
Photo Stylists: Tammy Liechty,
Tammy Steiner

ISBN: 978-1-59217-346-4

1 2 3 4 5 6 7 8 9